The Pocket Guide Of Golf Rules

Golf Rules Simplified

Anthony A. Blunden

Watchwood Publishing

While writing *The Pocket Guide Of Golf Rules,* I have received unlimited support from my wife, Barbara, my family and my friends. To each of them, I express my deepest appreciation.

Copyright 1994 by Anthony A. Blunden
All rights reserved
Printed in U.S.A.
Library of Congress Catalog 94-60710
ISBN 0-9641877-0-1

Illustrations by Laugh Lines
Walnut Creek, California
Lorraine Weidmark

Watchwood Publishing
P.O. Box 1387
Orinda, California 94563

Introduction

It's a fact. Golfers who know the Rules of the game have a distinct advantage over those who don't!

The United States Golf Association and the Royal and Ancient Golf Club of St. Andrews, Scotland, jointly write the *Rules of Golf,* the Rules which govern play throughout the world. These Rules are revised every fourth year, with the next revision scheduled for 1996.

As a golf addict, I have seen many golfers lose strokes, and even competitions, because they didn't know how to proceed properly in a given situation. As a Rules lecturer, I have had the opportunity to explain the various benefits and advantages that can be obtained by simply following the Rules.

Since many golfers don't have the time, or the inclination, to make a complete study of the Rules, I have compiled *The Pocket Guide Of Golf Rules*–a quick reference handbook which explains many of the Rules by using simple language, easy-to-follow diagrams, and humorous illustrations. As an added convenience, *The Pocket Guide* references the Official Rules and Appendix numbers.

It is my hope that *The Pocket Guide Of Golf Rules* will enhance your enjoyment of the Game of Golf while serving as a ready reference for any Rules questions which may arise.

Anthony A. Blunden

Table of Contents

Stroke Play And Match Play

STROKE PLAY AND MATCH PLAY DEFINED: Stroke Play, also sometimes known as Medal Play, is a competition based on the total number of strokes played. Match Play is a competition based on the number of holes won. The typical penalty in Stroke Play is *the loss of one or two strokes.* The typical penalty in Match Play is *the loss of the hole.* In a Stroke Play competition the other players are called Competitors, or Fellow-Competitors if playing in your group. In a Match Play competition the player or side you are competing against is called your Opponent.

You know, Barb... when we're competing in **STROKE PLAY** we're called **FELLOW-COMPETITORS.**

PROCEDURE WHEN YOU'RE UNSURE OF YOUR RIGHTS — IN STROKE PLAY COMPETITION (RULE 3-3):

In Stroke Play, if you become unsure of the proper way to proceed during play of a hole, continue play with your original ball using one alternative and also play a Second Ball from the point of uncertainty using another alternative. Before playing either ball from the point of uncertainty, tell the marker or one of your Fellow-Competitors what you're going to do and with which ball you want to score if the Rules will permit. If the score of your Second Ball is different from the score of your original ball, you must inform the tournament committee before returning your score card that you played a Second Ball, and why. The committee will then determine your final score for that hole. Note: A Second Ball is not a Provisional Ball.

PROCEDURE WHEN YOU'RE UNSURE OF YOUR RIGHTS — IN MATCH PLAY COMPETITION (RULE 2-5):

In Match Play, the playing of a Second Ball is not permitted. If you and your Opponent cannot reach agreement as to how an uncertainty should be resolved, and no committee member is available within a reasonable time, you have the right to play the hole under protest if you believe your Opponent is proceeding incorrectly. In order to preserve your right to present a *claim* to the tournament committee at the end of the round, you must tell your Opponent that you intend to make a claim at the end of the round, state the fact which you believe gives rise to the claim and indicate that you want the *Rules of Golf* to be applied. This information must be stated to your Opponent before either of you play from the Teeing Ground of the next hole, or, if it's the last hole, before you leave the Putting Green, otherwise the claim will not be considered by the tournament committee at the conclusion of the match.

<u>ADDITIONAL POINTERS:</u> (1) In Match Play, you are *dormie* when you are ahead by the same number of holes that remain to be played. (2) In Match Play, if you incur a penalty after you have holed out and your Opponent is left with a stroke to tie the hole, the hole is tied.

Equipment

EQUIPMENT DEFINED: Everything you use, wear and carry with you on the golf course is considered to be your Equipment, except your ball marker and the ball(s) you are playing on the hole you are playing. When you share a golf cart, the cart and everything in it are considered to be your Equipment unless the cart is being moved by the player sharing the cart, in which case the moving cart and everything in it are considered to be the Equipment of the other player.

Procedure When Your Ball Hits Your Equipment
(Rule 19-2): In Stroke Play, if your ball In Play hits your Equipment, you will incur *a two-stroke penalty.* In Match Play, if your ball In Play hits your Equipment, you will *lose the hole.*

Procedure Regarding Fourteen Club Limit (Rule 4-4): As part of your Equipment, you are permitted to carry a maximum of fourteen clubs during your round. You may share clubs, but only with your partner, and only if you have no more than fourteen clubs *in total* between you. In Stroke Play, you will incur *a two-stroke penalty* for each hole played with more than fourteen clubs, with a maximum penalty of four strokes per round. In Match Play, the score of the match is adjusted after play is finished on the hole where the breach is discovered. *One hole is then deducted* from the score of the offending player for each hole played with more than fourteen clubs, with a maximum deduction of two holes per round.

ADDITIONAL POINTERS: (1) As soon as you discover that you're carrying more than fourteen clubs, announce which ones are extra and take them out of play. If you use the extra clubs during the remainder of the round, you will be disqualified. (2) You are not permitted to

**E
Q
U
I
P
M
E
N
T**

change clubs in the middle of a round. However, if a club becomes unfit in the normal course of play during a round, or if you start with less than fourteen clubs, you may replace or add the proper number of additional clubs. The additional clubs may not be borrowed from those being used by another player on the course.

Teeing Ground

TEEING GROUND DEFINED: The Teeing Ground is a rectangular area which is located at the start of each hole. The front and sides of the rectangular area are defined by imaginary lines which run along the outside portions of the tee-markers. The distance from the front line of the Teeing Ground to the back line of the Teeing Ground is two club-lengths. Your ball is within the Teeing Ground if any part of your ball is within this rectangular area.

> Well, Bob...is my ball within the TEEING GROUND?

PROCEDURE FOR PLAYING FROM THE TEEING GROUND

[RULE 11-4]: In Stroke Play, your ball must be located within the Teeing Ground when you play your first stroke on each hole. If your ball is located outside the Teeing Ground when you play your first stroke, the strokes played with that ball are not counted. Instead, you must start over by playing another ball from within the Teeing Ground, with *a two-stroke penalty.* Thus, you will be hitting three. Also in Stroke Play, if you start play of a hole with a ball located outside the Teeing Ground, and then fail to correct your mistake before beginning play on the next hole, or, in the case of the final hole, if you leave the Putting Green before declaring your intention to correct your mistake on that hole, you will be *disqualified.* In Match Play, if your ball is located outside the Teeing Ground when you play your first stroke, there is *no penalty.* However, your Opponent may either accept your shot or immediately require you to cancel the stroke, and instead have you replay a first stroke with a ball located within the Teeing Ground.

<u>ADDITIONAL POINTERS:</u> (1) You may stand outside the Teeing Ground to hit a ball located within it. (2) Your ball is In Play as soon as you play a stroke from the Teeing Ground, even if you fail to hit your ball during

your stroke. (3) If you accidentally knock your ball off the tee before it is In Play, or if your ball falls off the tee before it is In Play, simply replace your ball, *without penalty.* (4) If your ball, In Play, falls off the tee after you Address it but before you begin your stroke, you must replace your ball, and take *a one-stroke penalty.* (5) If your ball, In Play, falls off the tee before you Address it, and due to no action on your part, you must play your ball where it comes to rest, *without penalty.*

Order Of Play

ORDER OF PLAY DEFINED: The Order Of Play specifies when it is a player's turn to play.

PROCEDURE FOR DETERMINING THE ORDER OF PLAY
(RULE 10): Unless specified in advance, the Order Of Play on the first Teeing Ground is usually decided by the toss of a coin or the flip of a tee. Thereafter, the player with the lowest gross score on the hole in Stroke Play, or the side that wins the hole in Match Play, has the *honors* and plays first on the next tee. The Order Of Play on the next tee remains the same when there is a tie. After the tee shots have been played, the player farthest from the hole plays first. If two balls are equidistant from the hole, decide the Order of Play by the toss of a coin or the flip of a tee.

PROCEDURE IF YOU ACCIDENTALLY PLAY OUT OF TURN
(RULE 10): In Stroke Play, if you accidentally play out of turn, there is *no penalty.* Similarly, in Match Play, if you play a stroke when it's your Opponent's turn, there is *no penalty.* However, in Match Play, your Opponent may either accept your shot or immediately require you to cancel the stroke and instead have you replay the stroke when it's your turn.

ADDITIONAL POINTERS: (1) You will be playing out of turn if you play either a Provisional Ball or a Second Ball from the Teeing Ground before your Fellow-Competitor in Stroke Play, or Opponent in Match Play,

has played a first stroke. Thus, if after playing your first stroke it appears that your ball might be Lost outside a Water Hazard or might be Out Of Bounds, you will be playing out of turn if you play a Provisional Ball before your Fellow-Competitor or your Opponent has played a first stroke. (2) In Stroke Play, you may be disqualified if you seek to gain an advantage by intentionally playing out of turn. (3) In a Four-Ball Match, balls belonging to the same side may be played in whatever order the side wishes.

Playing The Ball As It Lies

AS IT LIES DEFINED: One of the basic principles in Golf is that you should play both the ball and the course as you find them, unless the Rules provide otherwise. In other words, after you have played a stroke and your ball has come to rest, there should be no unauthorized modification of the Lie Of The Ball, your Line Of Play to the hole, or the Area Of Your Intended Swing before you play your next stroke.

It is *a two-stroke penalty* in Stroke Play, and *a loss of the hole* in Match Play, to:

1. *Improve Your Lie.* You are not permitted to use your foot, club, or anything else to press down grass, soil, sand or other irregularities that are behind or near your ball, except when teeing your ball on the Teeing Ground. When your ball is outside a Sand Bunker or Water Hazard and you are At Address, you are permitted to set your clubhead on the ground behind your ball, but you may not press your clubhead into the ground.

2. *Improve Your Line Of Play.* You are not permitted to bend, break or remove anything that is fixed or growing in order to Improve Your Line Of Play to the hole. However, you are permitted to remove Movable Obstructions on your Line Of Play. You are also permitted to remove Loose Impediments on your Line Of Play, as long as both your ball and the Loose Impediments are not in the same Sand Bunker or Water Hazard.

3. *Improve The Area Of Your Intended Swing.* You are not permitted to bend, break, or remove anything that is fixed or growing in order to Improve The Area Of Your Intended Swing. Thus, if you Improve The Area Of Your Intended Swing by knocking down leaves, or even just one leaf, during your practice swing, you will

— 14 —

be penalized. You will also be penalized if you Improve The Area Of Your Intended Swing by wrapping branches around each other or by standing on them. Note: You are permitted to *fairly* take your stance and to *reasonably* make a stroke. In other words, there is no penalty if some branches bend or break while you are backing into a bush or tree in order to get in position to fairly play a stroke or if they bend or break while you are reasonably taking your backswing or downswing.

Playing From Sand Bunkers
And Water Hazards

HAZARD DEFINED: A Hazard is a Sand Bunker or a Water Hazard.

PROCEDURE FOR PLAYING FROM SAND BUNKERS AND WATER HAZARDS (RULE 13): When your ball is in a Sand Bunker or a Water Hazard, it is *a two-stroke penalty* in Stroke Play, and *a loss of the hole* in Match Play, to:

1. *Ground Your Club.* Your club may not touch the ground in a Sand Bunker, or the ground or water in a Water Hazard, when you take a practice swing or when you take your backswing during your actual swing. Your club may touch long grass and other vegetation in a Water Hazard when you are making a practice swing, or during the backswing of your actual swing, as long as you don't improve your lie or ground your club while doing so. You may ground your club in any *grass-covered* area which is around and within a Sand Bunker since the grass-covered portion is not considered to be part of the Sand Bunker. Note: There is no penalty if your club touches the ground or water in a Hazard when you are attempting to prevent a fall.

2. *Move Loose Impediments.* You are not permitted to touch or move Loose Impediments, such as leaves, twigs or pebbles, that are lying in or are touching the Sand Bunker or Water Hazard where your ball is located, except when searching for a Lost Ball. Once you have located a ball in the Sand Bunker or Water Hazard, you are not permitted to remove additional Loose Impediments in order to identify the owner of the ball since there is no penalty for playing a Wrong Ball from a Sand Bunker or a Water Hazard.

3. *Test The Ground Condition.* You are not permitted to test the ground condition of the Hazard your ball is in or the ground condition of a similar Hazard. You

are permitted to set your extra clubs or the rake down in a Sand Bunker or Water Hazard, as long as you don't test the sand or soil by doing so. You are also permitted to smooth out the sand or soil after making a stroke in the Sand Bunker or Water Hazard, even if your ball is still in the Hazard, as long as you don't Improve Your Lie or get some benefit for subsequent play of the hole.

4. *Improve Your Lie.* You are not permitted to Improve The Lie of your ball. However, you are permitted to remove Movable Obstructions, such as movable Water Hazard stakes, bottles and rakes, even if your ball lies in the Sand Bunker or Water Hazard. If your ball moves as a result of removing the Obstruction, replace your ball in its original location, *without penalty.*

5. *Delay A Stroke.* You are not permitted to delay making a stroke to allow the wind or current to move your ball to a better spot in a Water Hazard.

ADDITIONAL POINTERS: (1) In both Stroke Play and Match Play, you will incur *a one-stroke penalty* if you touch or lift a ball to identify it when it is located in a Sand Bunker or a Water Hazard. (2) When your ball is in a Sand Bunker, you are entitled to Casual Water, Unplayable Lie, Burrowing Animal and Immovable Obstruction relief. You are not entitled to such relief when your ball is in a Water Hazard. Instead, you must proceed under the Water Hazard Rules. (3) There is no

Embedded Ball relief when your ball is in a Sand Bunker or a Water Hazard. (4) If you take several practice swings in a Sand Bunker or Water Hazard before playing your ball, and touch the ground each time, the penalty in Stroke Play is the *loss of two strokes in total,* not the loss of two strokes for each practice swing.

Lost Ball (Penalty)

This section is not applicable to:

1. A ball lost in a Water Hazard–see Water Hazard Options, page 36; or

2. A ball lost in Casual Water, in Ground Under Repair, a Burrowing Animal Disturbance, or in an Immovable Obstruction–see Lost Ball (No Penalty), page 24.

You'll have a LOST BALL if you can't find it within 5 minutes, Bob.

LOST BALL DEFINED (RULE 27): Your original ball will be a Lost Ball if:

1. You can't identify your original ball when you find it or you can't find it within five minutes after your side begins searching for it; or

2. You put another ball In Play before finding your original ball, even though you have not searched for your original ball for the full five minutes, or at all; or

3. You play your Provisional Ball from a place where the original ball is likely to be or from a point nearer the hole than that place.

PROCEDURE WHEN YOU HAVE A LOST BALL — OUTSIDE A WATER HAZARD (RULE 27): The penalty for a Lost Ball, in both Stroke Play and Match Play, is *the loss of one stroke and distance.* Thus, when your original ball is Lost, you must drop another ball as close as possible to the spot where you last hit your original ball, no nearer the hole. For example, if you can't find your original ball after hitting your second shot, you must drop and hit another ball from where you hit your second shot, but instead of hitting three you will be hitting four since your third stroke is a penalty stroke. If your original ball was hit from the Teeing Ground, you may tee and hit another ball from anywhere within the Teeing Ground.

Procedure For Playing A Provisional Ball (Rule 27):

When there is a reasonable possibility that your original ball is Lost *outside* a Water Hazard or is Out of Bounds, you may play a Provisional Ball to save time. The Provisional Ball must be played before you and your partner leave the hitting area and before your side begins searching for your original ball. Before playing a Provisional Ball, you must specifically announce that you are going to play a Provisional Ball and indicate how it can be distinguished from your original ball. Then, when it's your turn to play, drop your Provisional Ball as close as possible to the spot where you last played your original ball, no nearer the hole. If you last played your original ball from the Teeing Ground, you may tee and play your Provisional Ball from anywhere within the Teeing Ground. You may continue to play the Provisional Ball until you reach the place where your original ball is likely to be. Then, if you find your original ball in bounds, pick up the Provisional Ball and continue play with your original ball, *without penalty.* However, if you are unable to find your original ball, continue play with the Provisional Ball, making it your ball In Play, with a penalty of *one stroke and distance.* Once your Provisional Ball becomes the ball In Play, you must continue to play the hole with it, even if you later find your original ball.

Since that might end up being a **LOST BALL,** you may want to hit a **PROVISIONAL BALL,** Molly.

ADDITIONAL POINTERS: (1) You are not required to search for a Lost Ball for a full five minutes, or for any time at all, before putting another ball In Play. However, if you find your original ball in bounds before the five minute period has expired and before you put another ball In Play, the original ball remains your ball In Play, even if it's in an undesirable location, and even if you have orally declared it to be Lost. (2) If you can't identify your ball, it will be deemed to be a Lost Ball. Therefore, always put an identification mark on your ball. (3) If your ball is lost in a Water Hazard, proceed under the Water Hazard Rules rather than the Rules for a Lost Ball.

Lost Ball (No Penalty)

LOST BALL (NO PENALTY) DEFINED: You have a Lost Ball that is applicable to this section if there is *reasonable evidence* to indicate that your ball is lost, in bounds, in one of the following four Problem Areas:
1. Casual Water
2. Ground Under Repair
3. A Burrowing Animal Disturbance
4. An Immovable Obstruction

Well, Mike...at least there's not always a penalty for a **LOST BALL**.

Determine the point where your ball last crossed the margin of the Problem Area. Find the closest spot (X) from this point, no nearer the hole, where you can take a stance without the Problem Area interfering with your ball, feet or swing. This spot must be outside a Sand Bunker or Water Hazard and cannot be on a Putting Green. Put a marker, such as a tee, in the ground to indicate where your ball would be located if you hit from this new stance. Now drop your ball, *without penalty,* within one club-length of the marker, no nearer the hole than where your ball last crossed the margin. Do not drop your ball into a Sand Bunker, a Water Hazard or onto a Putting Green.

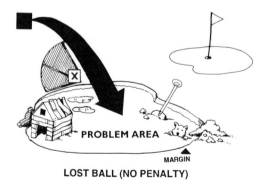

PROBLEM AREA

MARGIN

LOST BALL (NO PENALTY)

Procedure When Your Ball Is Lost In One Of The Four Problem Areas — In A Sand Bunker (Rule 24/25):

1. Drop a ball in the Sand Bunker, *without penalty*, as close as possible to the spot where your ball last crossed the margin of the Problem Area, on ground which affords maximum available relief from the condition, no nearer the hole; or

2. Drop a ball outside the Sand Bunker, with *a one-stroke penalty*. Imagine a straight line that goes from the hole to the spot where your ball last crossed the margin of the Problem Area. Continue to extend the line straight back from this spot and then drop your ball on the extended line, going as far back on the course as you want.

Procedure When Your Ball Is Lost In Ground Under Repair — In A Water Hazard (Rule 25):

1. Drop a ball in the Water Hazard, *without penalty*, as close as possible to the spot where your ball last crossed the margin of the Ground Under Repair, on ground which affords maximum available relief from the condition, no nearer the hole; or

2. Drop a ball outside the Water Hazard, with *a one-stroke penalty*. Imagine a straight line that goes from the hole to the spot where your ball last crossed the

margin of the Ground Under Repair. Continue to extend the line straight back from this spot and then drop your ball on the extended line, going as far back on the course as you want.

ADDITIONAL POINTERS: (1) If your ball is lost in a Water Hazard, there is no Casual Water, Burrowing Animal or Immovable Obstruction relief. Instead, you must proceed under the Water Hazard Rules. (2) If you decide your original ball is Lost and put another ball In Play, you may not later play your original ball if you find it in bounds.

Out Of Bounds

OUT OF BOUNDS DEFINED: Your ball is Out Of Bounds, and therefore out of play, when it comes to rest beyond markers which define the boundaries of the course. Out Of Bounds markers are often white stakes, white lines, fence posts, walls, railings and roads. When the boundary markers are stakes or fence posts, the Out Of Bounds line runs along the nearest inside points, e.g. the golf course side rather than the Out Of Bounds side, of the stakes or posts, at ground level. When the boundary is defined by a line on the ground, the line itself is Out Of Bounds. Your ball is in bounds unless all of it lies Out Of Bounds.

PROCEDURE WHEN YOUR BALL IS OUT OF BOUNDS (RULE 27): The penalty for hitting a ball Out of Bounds, in both Stroke Play and Match Play, is the loss of *one-stroke and distance.* When you hit a ball Out Of Bounds, you must drop another ball as close as possible to the spot where you last hit, no nearer the hole. For example, if you hit your ball Out Of Bounds on your third shot, you must drop and hit another ball from where you hit your third shot, but instead of hitting four you will be hitting five since your fourth stroke is a penalty stroke. If your original ball was hit from the Teeing Ground, you may tee and hit another ball from anywhere within the Teeing Ground.

PROCEDURE FOR PLAYING A PROVISIONAL BALL (RULE 27): When there is a reasonable possibility that your original ball is Out Of Bounds or is Lost *outside* a Water Hazard, you may play a Provisional Ball to save time. The Provisional Ball must be played before you and your partner leave the hitting area and before your side begins searching for your original ball. Before playing a Provisional Ball, you must specifically announce that you are going to play a Provisional Ball and indicate how it can be distinguished from your original ball.

Then, when it's your turn to play, drop your Provisional Ball as close as possible to the spot where you last played your original ball, no nearer the hole. If you last played your original ball from the Teeing Ground, you may tee and play your Provisional Ball from anywhere within the Teeing Ground. You may continue to play the Provisional Ball until you reach the place where your original ball is likely to be. Then, if you discover that your original ball is in bounds, pick up the Provisional Ball and continue play with your original ball, *without penalty*. However, if you discover that your original ball is Out Of Bounds, or is a Lost Ball, continue play with the Provisional Ball, making it your ball In Play, with a penalty of *one stroke and distance.* Once your

Provisional Ball becomes the ball In Play, you must continue to play the hole with it, even if you later find that your original ball is in bounds.

ADDITIONAL POINTERS: (1) If an Out Of Bounds marker for the hole you are playing interferes with your stance or swing when your ball is in bounds, you either have to play your ball as it lies or declare an Unplayable Lie. (2) You will incur *a two-stroke penalty* in Stroke Play, and *the loss of the hole* in Match Play, if you remove an Out Of Bounds marker. (3) You may stand Out Of Bounds to play a ball that is located in bounds.

O
U
T

O
F

B
O
U
N
D
S

Unplayable Lies

UNPLAYABLE LIE DEFINED: If you are unable to hit your ball, or, if, for any reason, you simply choose not to hit it from its present location, you may declare an Unplayable Lie, except when your ball is in a Water Hazard.

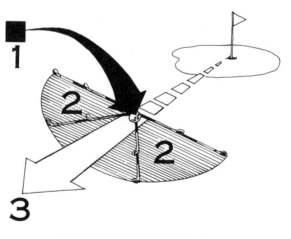

UNPLAYABLE LIE OPTIONS

PROCEDURE FOR RELIEF FROM AN UNPLAYABLE LIE — WHEN YOUR BALL IS OUTSIDE A SAND BUNKER AND OUTSIDE A WATER HAZARD AND NOT ON A PUTTING GREEN (RULE 28):

1. Drop your ball, *with a one-stroke penalty*, as close as possible to the spot where you last played a stroke, no nearer the hole. Note: If you last played a stroke from the Putting Green, place your ball. If you last played a stroke from the Teeing Ground, you may drop or re-tee your ball anywhere within the Teeing Ground; or

2. Drop your ball, *with a one-stroke penalty*, within two club-lengths of where your ball is located, no nearer the hole; or

3. Imagine a straight line that goes from the hole to where your ball is located in the Unplayable Lie. Continue to extend the line straight back from where your ball is located and then drop your ball on the extended line, *with a one-stroke penalty*, going as far back on the course as you want.

PROCEDURE FOR RELIEF FROM AN UNPLAYABLE LIE — WHEN YOUR BALL IS IN A SAND BUNKER (RULE 28):

1. Drop your ball, *with a one-stroke penalty*, as close as possible to the spot where you last played a stroke, no nearer the hole; or

2. Drop your ball in the Sand Bunker, *with a one-stroke penalty,* within two club-lengths of where your ball is located, no nearer the hole; or

3. Imagine a straight line that goes from the hole to where your ball is located in the Unplayable Lie. Continue to extend the line straight back from where your ball is located and then drop your ball on that extended line, *with a one-stroke penalty,* going as far back as you want, but staying within the Sand Bunker.

You could declare an **UNPLAYABLE LIE,** Bob!

PROCEDURE FOR RELIEF FROM AN UNPLAYABLE LIE —
WHEN YOUR BALL IS ABOVE THE GROUND (RULE 28): If
your ball has come to rest above the ground, in a bush or
tree for example, and you elect to proceed under the
two club-length option, first determine a spot on the
ground that is directly below your ball. Then drop your
ball, *with a one-stroke penalty,* within two club-lengths
of that spot, no nearer the hole.

ADDITIONAL POINTERS: (1) Be careful when you drop
your ball since you are not always entitled to a re-drop,
without penalty. For example, if you take a drop from an
Unplayable Lie and your ball rolls less than two-club
lengths, no nearer the hole, and into another Unplayable
Lie, you are not allowed to re-drop it without penalty.
Instead you must proceed, once again, under the Rules
for an Unplayable Lie. (2) If your ball is in a Water
Hazard, there is no Unplayable Lie relief. Instead you
must proceed under the Water Hazard Rules. (3) You
may clean your ball whenever it is lifted from an
Unplayable Lie. (4) You may use any club when measuring two club-lengths from the location of your ball.

U
N
P
L
A
Y
A
B
L
E

L
I
E
S

Water Hazard Options

WATER HAZARD DEFINED: If your ball is in a lake, pond, river, ditch or surface drainage ditch, it is in a Water Hazard, even if it is not in water. Water Hazards are either *Regular* Water Hazards, usually known simply as Water Hazards, or Lateral Water Hazards. *Regular* Water Hazards are generally defined by yellow stakes or lines and usually have three options of play. Lateral Water Hazards are generally defined by red stakes or lines and usually have five options of play.

The stakes and lines which are used as markers to define the margins of the Water Hazard are themselves part of the Water Hazard. Your ball is in the Water Hazard if any part of it crosses the margin of the Water Hazard.

Uh, Mike...there are other options of play from a WATER HAZARD, you know.

Procedure When Your Ball Lies In, Touches Or Is Lost In A Regular Water Hazard (Rule 26):

1. Play your ball as it lies, *without penalty;* or

2. Drop a ball, *with a one-stroke penalty,* as close as possible to the spot where you last played a stroke, no nearer the hole. Note: If you last played from the Teeing Ground, you may re-tee your ball; or

3. Determine the spot where your ball last crossed the margin of the Water Hazard. Imagine a straight line that goes from the hole to that spot. Continue to extend the line straight back from that spot and then drop your ball, *with a one-stroke penalty,* behind the Water Hazard and on the extended line, going as far back on the course as you want.

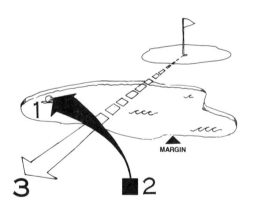

**"REGULAR" WATER HAZARD OPTIONS
(YELLOW STAKES)**

Procedure When Your Ball Lies In, Touches Or Is Lost In A Lateral Water Hazard (Rule 26):

1. Play your ball as it lies, *without penalty;* or

2. Drop a ball, *with a one-stroke penalty,* as close as possible to the spot where you last played a stroke, no nearer the hole. Note: If you last played from the Teeing Ground, you may re-tee your ball; or

3. Determine the spot where your ball last crossed the margin of the Water Hazard. Imagine a straight line that goes from the hole to that spot. Continue to extend the line straight back from that spot and then drop your ball, *with a one-stroke penalty,* behind the Water Hazard and on the extended line, going as far back on the course as you want; or

4. Drop a ball, *with a one-stroke penalty,* outside the Water Hazard and within two club-lengths of where your ball last crossed the margin of the Hazard, no nearer the hole. Note: When using this option, it is permissible to drop your ball on the Putting Green; or

5. Drop a ball, *with a one-stroke penalty,* on the opposite side of the Water Hazard. When using this option, you must first determine the distance from the hole to the spot where your ball last crossed the margin of the Water Hazard. Next, find a spot on the margin on the other side of the Water Hazard that is equidistant from the hole. Finally, drop your ball outside the Water

Hazard, within two club-lengths of this new spot, no nearer the hole.

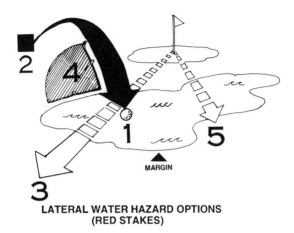

LATERAL WATER HAZARD OPTIONS
(RED STAKES)

PROCEDURE FOR PLAYING FROM DROP AREAS (APP.I):
Occasionally a specially marked Drop Area is provided as an additional option of play from a Water Hazard. If you elect to proceed by using this option, drop your ball, *with a one-stroke penalty,* anywhere within the Drop Area. Thus, if your ball entered the Water Hazard on your third stroke, you will be hitting five from the Drop Area. Note that if your ball rolls out of the Drop Area and comes to rest within two club-lengths of where it first hit the ground in the Drop Area, no nearer the hole, and not in a Sand Bunker or a Water Hazard, or on a Putting Green, it will be In Play.

Too bad, Mike...but you can't play a PROVISIONAL BALL since your original ball is definitely in the WATER HAZARD.

PROCEDURE REGARDING PLAY OF A PROVISIONAL BALL WHEN YOUR ORIGINAL BALL IS IN A WATER HAZARD (RULE 27-2):

Unless there is a Local Rule to the contrary, you may play a Provisional Ball only when there is a reasonable possibility that your original ball is lost *outside* a Water Hazard or is Out Of Bounds. If you *know* that your original ball is in a Water Hazard, you are not permitted to play a Provisional Ball. If you do play a Provisional Ball when your original ball is definitely in the Water Hazard, your original ball will be considered a Lost Ball and the *Provisional Ball* will become your ball In Play, *with a penalty of one stroke and distance.*

PROCEDURE WHEN A BALL PLAYED FROM WITHIN A WATER HAZARD BECOMES LOST OUTSIDE A WATER HAZARD OR GOES OUT OF BOUNDS (RULE 26-2):

1. Determine the spot where the ball last crossed the margin of the Hazard, before it came to rest in the Hazard, and imagine a straight line that goes from the hole to that spot. Continue to extend the line straight back from that spot and then drop your ball behind the Water Hazard and on the extended line, going as far back on the course as you want. Under this option you will incur *a one-stroke penalty* for your Lost or Out Of Bounds ball as well as *an additional one-stroke penalty;* or

2. Drop a ball as close as possible to the spot where your ball was located when you last played it from outside the Water Hazard, no nearer the hole. Under this option you will incur *a one-stroke penalty* for your Lost or Out Of Bounds ball as well as *an additional one-stroke penalty;* or

3. Drop a ball, *with a one-stroke penalty,* as close as possible to the spot where your ball was located when you last played it from inside the Water Hazard, no nearer the hole. Note: If you don't like your drop when using this option, you may lift your ball before playing it, and then drop it where mentioned above in options 1 or 2, *adding another penalty stroke.*

Procedure When A Ball Played From Within A Water Hazard Remains In The Hazard (Rule 26-2):

1. Play the ball as it lies, *without penalty;* or

2. Drop a ball, *with a one-stroke penalty,* as close as possible to the spot where your ball was located when you last played it from Outside the Water Hazard, no nearer the hole; or

3. Determine the spot where the ball last crossed the margin of the Water Hazard and imagine a straight line that goes from the hole to the spot. Continue to extend the line straight back from the spot and then drop your ball behind the Water Hazard and on the extended line, *with a one-stroke penalty,* going as far back on the course as you want; or

4. Drop a ball, *with a one-stroke penalty,* as close as possible to the spot where your ball was located when you last played it from Inside the Water Hazard, no nearer the hole. Note: If you don't like your drop when using this option, you may lift your ball before playing it, and then drop it where mentioned above in options 2 or 3, *adding another penalty stroke.*

Additional Pointers: (1) If you lose your ball, you must proceed under the Rules relating to a Lost Ball (Penalty) unless there is *reasonable evidence* to indicate that your ball is actually lost in the Water Hazard.

(2) If a movable Water Hazard stake interferes with your ball, stance or swing, you may remove the stake, *without penalty*, even if your ball is in the Water Hazard. If the Water Hazard stake is immovable, you are entitled to Immovable Obstruction relief only if your ball is located outside the Water Hazard. You must proceed under the Water Hazard Rules if your ball lies within the Water Hazard. (3) If your ball lies in or touches a Water Hazard, there is no Casual Water, Embedded Ball, Unplayable Lie, Burrowing Animal, Or Immovable Obstruction relief. Instead you must proceed under the Water Hazard Rules. (4) When you are permitted to lift your ball in a Water Hazard, you may clean it before dropping it. (5) To properly play your ball from a Water Hazard, refer to the section entitled Playing From Sand Bunkers and Water Hazards, page 16.

Relief From Burrowing Animal
Disturbances

BURROWING ANIMALS DEFINED: Some reptiles, some birds and some animals live in holes they make in the ground. Collectively these creatures are referred to as Burrowing Animals. A hole, cast, or a runway made by a Burrowing Animal is referred to as a Burrowing Animal Disturbance.

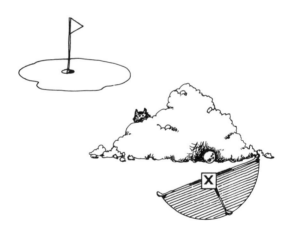

BURROWING ANIMAL RELIEF

<u>*PROCEDURE FOR RELIEF — GENERALLY (RULE 24-1):*</u>
You are entitled to relief if your ball lies in or touches a Burrowing Animal Disturbance or if a Burrowing Animal Disturbance interferes with your stance or the area of your intended swing, or Line Of Putt when your ball is on the Putting Green. It is important to note, however, that there is no such relief when there is interference caused by a nonburrowing creature such as a dog, a deer or a raccoon. If your ball becomes lost in a Burrowing Animal Disturbance, see Lost Ball (No Penalty), page 24.

<u>*PROCEDURE FOR RELIEF FROM INTERFERENCE CAUSED BY A BURROWING ANIMAL DISTURBANCE — OUTSIDE A SAND BUNKER AND OUTSIDE A WATER HAZARD AND NOT ON A PUTTING GREEN (RULE 25-1):*</u>
1. Play your ball as it lies, *without penalty;* or

2. Lift, clean and drop your ball, *without penalty,* within one club-length of the *nearest point of relief.* To determine the *nearest point of relief,* find the closest spot (X) from your ball, no nearer the hole, where you can take a stance without the Disturbance interfering with your ball, feet or swing. This spot must be outside a Sand Bunker or Water Hazard and not on a Putting Green. Put a marker, such as a tee, in the ground to indicate where your ball would be located if you hit from

this new stance. Now, drop your ball within one club-length of the marker, no nearer the hole than where your ball was at rest. Do not drop your ball into a Sand Bunker, a Water Hazard or onto a Putting Green.

PROCEDURE FOR RELIEF FROM INTERFERENCE CAUSED BY A BURROWING ANIMAL DISTURBANCE — IN A SAND BUNKER (RULE 25-1):

1. Play your ball as it lies, *without penalty;* or

2. Lift, clean, and then drop your ball back into the Sand Bunker, *without penalty.* Drop your ball as near as possible to the spot where it was originally at rest, no nearer the hole, and on ground which provides maximum relief from the Disturbance; or

3. Lift, clean and then drop your ball outside the Sand Bunker, *with a one-stroke penalty.* Imagine a straight line that goes from the hole to the spot where your ball came to rest in the Sand Bunker. Continue to extend the line straight back from that spot and then drop your ball on that extended line, going as far back on the course as you want.

PROCEDURE FOR RELIEF FROM INTERFERENCE CAUSED BY A BURROWING ANIMAL DISTURBANCE ON THE PUTTING GREEN — WHEN YOUR BALL IS ON THE PUTTING GREEN (RULE 25-1):

1. Play your ball as it lies, *without penalty;* or

2. Lift, clean and then place your ball, *without penalty,* at the nearest point which provides maximum available relief from the Disturbance, and where the Disturbance is not in your Line Of Putt, no nearer the hole, and not in a Sand Bunker or Water Hazard. Note that the nearest point may be located off the Putting Green.

ADDITIONAL POINTERS: (1) You are not entitled to relief from a Burrowing Animal Disturbance if you have to use an unnecessarily abnormal stance, swing, or direction of play before there is interference, or if the ball is clearly unplayable because of interference by something from which free relief is not available, such as a tree. (2) Your ball must be on the Putting Green in order to get relief from a Burrowing Animal Disturbance which is on your Line Of Putt on the Putting Green. (3) If your ball is in a Water Hazard, there is no relief from a Burrowing Animal Disturbance. Instead you must proceed under the Water Hazard Rules.

BURROWING ANIMAL DISTURBANCES

Relief From Casual Water

CASUAL WATER DEFINED: Casual Water is a temporary accumulation of water which is anywhere on the course, except in a Water Hazard. It must be visible before or after you take your stance. In practice, if there is enough *accumulation of water* to ooze up over the soles of your shoes while taking your stance, you are in Casual Water. Snow and natural ice may be treated as either Casual Water or Loose Impediments. Dew and frost are not considered Casual Water, and manufactured ice is an Obstruction rather than Casual Water.

CASUAL WATER RELIEF

PROCEDURE FOR RELIEF — GENERALLY: You are enti-tled to relief if your ball lies in or touches Casual Water or if Casual Water interferes with your stance or the area of your intended swing, or Line Of Putt when your ball is on the Putting Green. If your ball becomes lost in Casual Water, see Lost Ball (No Penalty), page 24.

PROCEDURE FOR RELIEF FROM INTERFERENCE CAUSED BY CASUAL WATER — OUTSIDE A SAND BUNKER AND OUTSIDE A WATER HAZARD AND NOT ON A PUTTING GREEN (RULE 25-1):

1. Play your ball as it lies, _without penalty;_ or

2. Lift, clean and drop your ball, _without penalty,_ within one club-length of the _nearest point of relief._ To determine the _nearest point of relief,_ find the closest spot (X) from your ball, no nearer the hole, where you can take a stance without the Casual Water interfering with your ball, feet or swing. This spot must be outside a Sand Bunker or Water Hazard and not on a Putting Green. Put a marker, such as a tee, in the ground to indi-cate where your ball would be located if you hit from this new stance. Now, drop your ball within one club-length of the marker, no nearer the hole than where your ball was at rest. Do not drop your ball into a Sand Bunker, a Water Hazard or onto a Putting Green.

PROCEDURE FOR RELIEF FROM INTERFERENCE CAUSED BY CASUAL WATER — IN A SAND BUNKER (RULE 25-1):

1. Play your ball as it lies, *without penalty;* or

2. Lift, clean and then drop your ball back into the Sand Bunker, *without penalty.* Drop your ball as near as possible to the spot where it was originally at rest, no nearer the hole, and on ground which provides maximum relief from the Casual Water; or

3. Lift, clean and then drop your ball outside the Sand Bunker, *with a one-stroke penalty.* Imagine a straight line that goes from the hole to the spot where your ball came to rest in the Sand Bunker. Continue to extend the line straight back from that spot and then drop your ball on that extended line, going as far back on the course as you want.

PROCEDURE FOR RELIEF FROM INTERFERENCE CAUSED BY CASUAL WATER ON THE PUTTING GREEN — WHEN YOUR BALL IS ON THE PUTTING GREEN (RULE 25-1):

1. Play your ball as it lies, *without penalty;* or

2. Lift, clean and then place your ball, *without penalty,* at the nearest point which provides maximum available relief from the Casual Water, and where the Casual Water is not in your Line Of Putt, no nearer the hole, and not in a Sand Bunker or Water Hazard. Note that the nearest point may be off the Putting Green.

ADDITIONAL POINTERS: (1) You are not entitled to relief from interference caused by Casual Water if you have to use an unnecessarily abnormal stance, swing or direction of play before there is interference, or if the ball is clearly unplayable because of interference by something from which free relief is not available, such as a tree. (2) Your ball must be on the Putting Green in order to get relief from Casual Water which is on your Line Of Putt on the Putting Green. (3) If your ball is in a Water Hazard, there is no Casual Water relief. Instead you must proceed under the Water Hazard Rules. (4) Since dew is not Casual Water or a Loose Impediment, you will incur a _two-stroke penalty_ in Stroke Play, and a _loss of the hole_ in Match Play, if you brush aside dew which is on your Line Of Putt on the Putting Green. (5) If you find your ball in a Sand Bunker which is completely covered by Casual Water, you may proceed by using one of the options mentioned above, or you may proceed under the Rules for an Unplayable Lie. (6) You are not entitled to Casual Water relief when your ball is in soft, mushy earth, unless water is visible on the surface before or after you take your stance.

Relief From An Embedded Ball

EMBEDDED BALL DEFINED: When a ball is plugged in its own pitch-mark, it is an Embedded Ball. A pitch-mark is a hole in the ground which is made by the impact of a ball.

PROCEDURE FOR RELIEF WHEN YOUR BALL IS EMBEDDED — OUTSIDE A SAND BUNKER AND OUTSIDE A WATER HAZARD (RULE 25-2): When you have an Embedded Ball in the fairway or any *closely mown area* of the course, and not in a Sand Bunker or Water Hazard, you may:

1. Play your ball as it lies, *without penalty;* or

2. Lift, clean, and then drop your ball, *without penalty,* as close as possible to the pitch-mark, no nearer the hole.

Note: All portions of the course, including paths through the rough, are considered *closely mown areas* when they are cut to the same height as a fairway, or less.

PROCEDURE FOR RELIEF WHEN YOUR BALL IS EMBEDDED — IN A SAND BUNKER OR A WATER HAZARD (RULE 25-2): When you have an Embedded Ball in a Sand Bunker, there is no Embedded Ball relief, and thus you must either play the ball as it lies or declare your ball Unplayable and proceed under the Rules for an Unplayable Lie. When you have an Embedded Ball in a Water Hazard, there is no Embedded Ball or Unplayable Lie relief, and thus you must proceed under the Water Hazard Rules.

EMBEDDED BALL

<u>ADDITIONAL POINTERS:</u> (1) When your ball is Embedded off the Putting Green, you are not allowed to repair your pitch-mark before dropping your ball. However, if you drop your ball and it rolls into the pitch-mark, you may re-drop it, *without penalty.* (2) If your ball is Embedded on the Putting Green, you may mark, lift and clean your ball, repair the pitch-mark, and then replace your ball, *without penalty.* (3) You may lift your ball, without penalty, to determine if it is Embedded. Before lifting your ball, make sure you advise a Fellow-Competitor or Marker in Stroke Play, or an Opponent in Match Play, of your intention to lift it, give them an opportunity to watch, and then mark your ball before lifting it. (4) You may clean your ball if it is Embedded and you take relief from the Embedded Lie. (5) If your ball becomes Embedded when you drop it pursuant to an applicable Rule, you may re-drop it. If it becomes Embedded when re-dropped, place your ball as close as possible to the spot where the ball Embedded on the re-drop, no nearer the hole.

Relief From Ground Under Repair

GROUND UNDER REPAIR DEFINED: Ground Under Repair includes any part of the course which the golf committee has marked as such, usually by white lines. Even if not marked, material piled for removal and holes made by the greenskeeper are considered Ground Under Repair, except holes made during an aerification process are not considered Ground Under Repair unless a Local Rule provides otherwise. Unmarked grass cuttings, miscellaneous clippings, and other materials which are not intended to be removed and which have been left and abandoned on the course are not Ground Under Repair. Similarly, bare patches, tracks, roads, paths, and shallow ruts or grooves made by maintenance vehicles are not Ground Under Repair, unless so marked.

PROCEDURE FOR RELIEF — GENERALLY (RULE 24-1): You are entitled to relief if your ball lies in or touches Ground Under Repair or if Ground Under Repair interferes with your stance or the area of your intended swing, or Line Of Putt when your ball is on the Putting Green. If your ball becomes lost in Ground Under Repair, see Lost Ball (No Penalty), page 24.

PROCEDURE FOR RELIEF FROM INTERFERENCE CAUSED BY GROUND UNDER REPAIR — OUTSIDE A SAND BUNKER AND OUTSIDE A WATER HAZARD AND NOT ON A PUTTING GREEN (RULE 25-1):

1. Play your ball as it lies, *without penalty;* or

2. Lift, clean and drop your ball, *without penalty,* within one club-length of the *nearest point of relief.* To determine the *nearest point of relief,* find the closest spot (X) from your ball, no nearer the hole, where you can take a stance without the Ground Under Repair interfering with your ball, feet or swing. This spot must be outside a Sand Bunker or Water Hazard and not on a Putting Green. Put a marker, such as a tee, in the ground to indicate where your ball would be located if you hit from this new stance. Now, drop your ball within one club-length of the marker, no nearer the hole than where your ball was at rest. Do not drop your ball into a Sand Bunker, a Water Hazard or onto a Putting Green.

PROCEDURE FOR RELIEF FROM INTERFERENCE CAUSED BY GROUND UNDER REPAIR — IN A SAND BUNKER OR IN A WATER HAZARD (RULE 25-1):

1. Play your ball as it lies, *without penalty;* or

2. Lift, clean and then drop your ball back into the Sand Bunker or Water Hazard, *without penalty.* Drop your ball as near as possible to the spot where it was

originally at rest, no nearer the hole, and on ground which provides maximum relief from the Ground Under Repair; or

3. Lift, clean and then drop your ball out of the Sand Bunker or Water Hazard, with *a one-stroke penalty.* Imagine a straight line that goes from the hole to the spot where your ball came to rest in the Sand Bunker or Water Hazard. Continue to extend the line straight back from that spot and then drop your ball on that extended line, going as far back on the course as you want.

GROUND UNDER REPAIR RELIEF

PROCEDURE FOR RELIEF FROM INTERFERENCE CAUSED BY GROUND UNDER REPAIR ON THE PUTTING GREEN — WHEN YOUR BALL IS ON THE PUTTING GREEN (RULE 25-1):

1. Play your ball as it lies, *without penalty;* or

2. Lift, clean and then place your ball, *without penalty,* at the nearest point which provides maximum available relief from the Ground Under Repair, and where the Ground Under Repair is not in your line of Putt, no nearer the hole, and not in a Sand Bunker or Water Hazard. Note that the nearest point may be located off the Putting Green.

ADDITIONAL POINTERS: (1) You are not entitled to relief from interference caused by Ground Under Repair if you have to use an unnecessarily abnormal stance, swing or direction of play before there is inter-ference, or if the ball is clearly unplayable because of interference by something from which free relief is not available, such as a tree. (2) Your ball must be on the Putting Green in order to get relief from Ground Under Repair which is on your Line Of Putt on the Putting Green. (3) A ball is in Ground Under Repair when any part of the ball touches the line that defines Ground Under Repair.

Relief From Loose Impediments

LOOSE IMPEDIMENTS DEFINED: Loose Impediments are objects made by nature, while Obstructions are objects made by man. By definition they cannot be (1) growing, (2) fixed to something, (3) solidly embedded, or (4) adhering to the ball. Worms and insects, and casts or heaps made by them, are considered to be Loose Impediments, but the dew on the grass is not. Examples of Loose Impediments are leaves, loose stones, aerification plugs, cut grass and twigs. Sand and loose soil are Loose Impediments only when they are on the Putting Green. Snow and natural ice may be treated as either Casual Water or Loose Impediments. Artificial ice is an Obstruction rather than a Loose Impediment.

PROCEDURE FOR RELIEF FROM LOOSE IMPEDIMENTS (RULE 23-1): If your ball is at rest, you are permitted to remove Loose Impediments such as twigs and leaves, *without penalty,* except when both your ball and the Loose Impediments lie in or touch the same Sand Bunker or Water Hazard. If your ball is In Play on the Putting Green and your ball moves as a direct result of removing Loose Impediments, replace your ball, *without penalty.* If your ball is off the Putting Green and you move your ball while you are in the process of removing Loose Impediments, or if you remove Loose Impediments within a club-length of your ball and your ball thereafter moves, you will incur *a one-stroke penalty.* You must also replace your ball before taking your next stroke, unless the movement of the ball occurs after you have begun your swing and you don't discontinue your swing. If you remove Loose Impediments when both your ball and the Loose Impediments are in the same Sand Bunker or Water Hazard, you will incur *a two-stroke penalty* in Stroke Play, and *the loss of the hole* in Match Play.

ADDITIONAL POINTERS: (1) Sand and loose soil are Loose Impediments only when they are on the Putting Green. Thus, you will incur *a two-stroke penalty* in Stroke Play, and *the loss of the hole* in Match Play, if you remove sand or loose soil from the apron or from some other location off the Putting Green. (2) You will incur *a two-stroke penalty* in Stroke Play, and *the loss of the hole* in Match Play, if, while a ball is in motion, you remove a Loose Impediment which might influence the movement of that ball.

Relief From Obstructions

OBSTRUCTIONS DEFINED: All man-made objects, including roads and paths made of artificial materials, are considered Obstructions, except: (1) objects which are used to define Out Of Bound boundaries, such as stakes, walls, fences and railings; (2) construction which is deemed by the golf committee to be an integral part of the course, and (3) parts of immovable artificial objects which are themselves Out Of Bounds.

Obstructions are either Movable or Immovable. Movable Obstructions, such as rakes, tin cans, movable Water Hazard stakes, and hoses, can be lifted and moved without unreasonable effort, without unduly delaying play, and without damaging the course. Immovable Obstructions, such as buildings, fences, cart paths, immovable Water Hazard stakes, and sprinkler heads, are fixed in place and obviously cannot be moved.

PROCEDURE FOR RELIEF — GENERALLY (RULE 24-1): When your ball is at rest, you may obtain relief from a Movable Obstruction by moving the Obstruction. When your ball is at rest, relief from an Immovable Obstruction is obtained by moving your ball. However, you are only entitled to Immovable Obstruction relief when your ball lies in or on the Immovable Obstruction, or when your ball lies so close to the Immovable Obstruction that it interferes with your stance, the area of your intended swing, or your line of putt when your ball is on the Putting Green.

PROCEDURE FOR RELIEF FROM A MOVABLE OBSTRUCTION — WHEN YOUR BALL ISN'T IN OR ON THE OBSTRUCTION (RULE 24-1): If you wish to obtain relief from a Movable Obstruction simply remove the Obstruction, *without penalty.* If your ball moves as a direct result of removing the Movable Obstruction, clean and then replace your ball, *without penalty.* This

relief is available even when your ball is in a Sand Bunker or a Water Hazard.

PROCEDURE FOR RELIEF FROM A MOVABLE OBSTRUCTION — WHEN YOUR BALL LIES IN OR ON THE OBSTRUCTION (RULE 24-1):
If your ball lies in or on a Movable Obstruction, such as a paper bag, lift the ball, remove the Obstruction, and then clean and drop the ball, or place the ball if it is on the Putting Green, *without penalty*, as close as possible to where the ball was at rest, no nearer the hole. This relief is available even when your ball is in a Sand Bunker or Water Hazard.

PROCEDURE FOR RELIEF FROM INTERFERENCE CAUSED BY AN IMMOVABLE OBSTRUCTION — WHEN YOUR BALL IS OUTSIDE A SAND BUNKER AND OUTSIDE A WATER HAZARD AND NOT ON A PUTTING GREEN (RULE 24-2):
If your ball lies in or on an Immovable Obstruction, or if your ball lies so close to the Immovable Obstruction that it interferes with your stance or the area of your intended swing, you are entitled to Immovable Obstruction relief. Lift, clean and drop your ball, *without penalty*, within one club-length of the *nearest point of relief*. To determine the *nearest point of relief*, find the closest spot (X) from your ball, no nearer the hole, where you can take a stance without the Obstruction interfering with your ball, feet and swing. This spot

must be outside a Sand Bunker and outside a Water Hazard and not on a Putting Green. (To find this closest spot from your ball you may not cross over, go through, or go under the Immovable Obstruction unless the ball lies in or on the Immovable Obstruction, or unless the Immovable Obstruction is a road or a cart path.) Put a marker, such as a tee, in the ground to indicate where

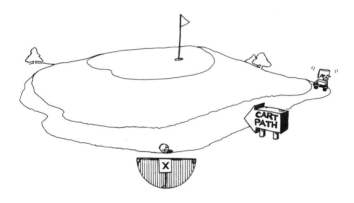

IMMOVABLE OBSTRUCTION RELIEF

your ball would be located if you hit from this new stance. Now, drop your ball within one club-length of the marker, no nearer the hole than where your ball was at rest. Do not drop your ball into a Sand Bunker, a Water Hazard or onto a Putting Green.

PROCEDURE FOR RELIEF FROM INTERFERENCE CAUSED BY AN IMMOVABLE OBSTRUCTION — WHEN YOUR BALL IS IN A SAND BUNKER (RULE 24-2):

Follow the relief mentioned above with the following exception: You must drop the ball, *without penalty,* back into the Sand Bunker.

PROCEDURE FOR RELIEF FROM INTERFERENCE CAUSED BY AN IMMOVABLE OBSTRUCTION — WHEN YOUR BALL IS ON A PUTTING GREEN (RULE 24-2):

If your ball is on the Putting Green and lies in or on an Immovable Obstruction, or so close to the Immovable Obstruction that it interferes with your stance, the area of your intended swing, or your line of Putt, you are entitled to Immovable Obstruction relief. You may lift, clean and then place your ball, *without penalty*, at the nearest point which affords relief from the Immovable Obstruction, no nearer the hole, and not in a Sand Bunker or Water Hazard. Note: The nearest point may be located off the Putting Green.

ADDITIONAL POINTERS: (1) There is no Immovable Obstruction relief when your ball is in a Water Hazard. Instead you must proceed under the Water Hazard Rules. (2) You are not entitled to relief from interference caused by an Immovable Obstruction if the Obstruction simply interferes with your line of flight to the hole, or you have to take an unnecessarily abnormal stance or swing before there is interference, or the ball is clearly unplayable because of interference by something from which free relief is not available, such as a tree. (3) You must use the club which you intend to hit with when determining the nearest point of relief from the Immovable Obstruction. However, you may use any club when measuring for a club-length drop. (4) When there is a possibility that your ball might move as a result of moving a Movable Obstruction, mark your ball before moving the Movable Obstruction so you will be able to replace your ball at the proper spot, if necessary.

Ball Deflection

BALL DEFLECTION DEFINED: If your moving ball is accidentally deflected or stopped as a result of coming in contact with someone or something other than a portion of the golf course, Ball Deflection has occurred. Whether or not there is relief or a penalty for this Ball Deflection depends on the circumstances.

Procedure When Your Moving Ball Hits You, Your Partner, Your Caddies Or Your Equipment

[Rule 19-2]: In Stroke Play, if your moving ball is accidentally deflected or stopped by you, your partner, your caddies or equipment, play your ball where it has come to rest, with *a two-stroke penalty.* If your ball has come to rest in or on your clothes or equipment, you must lift your ball, move the article of clothing or equipment, and then drop your ball, or place it if it is on the Putting Green, as close as possible to where it has come to rest, no nearer the hole. In Match Play, the penalty is *a loss of the hole.*

Procedure When Your Moving Ball Hits Your Opponent, Etc. [Rule 19-3]:

In Match Play, if your moving ball is accidentally deflected or stopped by your Opponent, your Opponent's caddie or their equipment, no one incurs a penalty. However, you may, at your option, play the ball where it has come to rest or replay the ball from where you last played a stroke. If you elect to play the ball from where it has come to rest and it is in or on their clothes or equipment, you may lift your ball, move the article of clothing or equipment, and then drop your ball, or place it if it is on the Putting Green, as close as possible to where it has come to rest, no nearer the hole.

BALL DEFLECTION

PROCEDURE WHEN YOUR MOVING BALL HITS A FELLOW-COMPETITOR OR AN OUTSIDE AGENCY, ETC.

[RULE 19-1]: If your moving ball is accidentally deflected or stopped during Stroke Play by a Fellow-Competitor, a Fellow-Competitor's caddie or their equipment, or during Stroke Play or Match Play by an Outside Agency such as a spectator or a greenskeeper, play your ball where it has come to rest, *without penalty.* Exceptions: (1) If you put your ball in motion from off the Putting Green and it has come to rest *in* or *on* a moving object, drop a ball at the location where the contact occurred between your ball and the moving object, or place it at that location if the contact occurred on the Putting Green. (2) If you put your ball in motion on the Putting Green and your ball is deflected or stopped by a Fellow-Competitor or an Outside Agency, except a worm or an insect, you must cancel the stroke and replay it.

PROCEDURE WHEN YOUR MOVING BALL HITS A BALL THAT IS AT REST *[RULE 19-5]:*

If your moving ball is deflected or stopped as a result of hitting a ball that is at rest, play your ball where it has come to rest and return the other ball to its original position. In Stroke Play, there is *no penalty* if your ball hits a ball that is at rest, unless both balls are on the Putting Green when you make your stroke, in which case you will incur *a two-stroke penalty.* In Match Play, there is *no penalty* if your ball hits your Opponent's ball at rest, even if both balls are on the Putting Green when you make your stroke.

PROCEDURE WHEN YOUR MOVING BALL HITS ANOTHER MOVING BALL (RULE 19-5): If your moving ball is deflected or stopped by another moving ball, play your ball where it has come to rest, *without penalty.* Exceptions: (1) In Stroke Play, if your moving ball hits your Fellow-Competitor's moving ball when both balls have been putted on the Putting Green, the player who putted out of turn will incur *a two-stroke penalty* and must play the ball where it has come to rest. The other player must replace the ball and replay the putt, *without penalty.* In Match Play, the player who played out of turn will *lose the hole.* (2) If you make a putt on the Putting Green and your moving ball comes in contact with a moving ball that has not come from your Fellow-Competitor or Opponent, you must replace your ball and replay your putt, *without penalty.*

ADDITIONAL POINTERS: If any player or caddie intentionally takes action to influence the position or movement of the ball, except in accordance with the Rules, there is *a two-stroke penalty* in Stroke Play, and *a loss of the hole* in Match Play.

— 71 —

Ball Movement

BALL MOVEMENT DEFINED: If your ball In Play has come to rest in one spot and then moves to another spot before you make another stroke, Ball Movement has occurred. Whether or not there is relief or a penalty for this Ball Movement depends on the circumstances.

PROCEDURE WHEN YOUR BALL MOVES — GENERAL RULES (RULE 18):

1. If your ball is at rest and you, your partners or your caddies touch, lift or move it, except when permitted by a Rule, or if your equipment hits and moves it, you will incur _a one-stroke penalty._ You must then replace your ball before playing your next stroke, unless the movement of the ball occurs after you have begun your swing and you don't discontinue your swing.

2. If your ball is at rest and an Outside Agency, such as a spectator, causes the ball to move, or if it is moved by another ball striking it, replace the ball _without penalty._

3. If your ball is at rest, replace it, _without penalty,_ if you accidentally move it as a direct result of:

a. Measuring which ball is furthest from the hole.

b. Searching for a ball lost in Casual Water, a

Burrowing Animal Disturbance, Ground Under Repair, or a Sand Bunker or a Water Hazard.

    c. Repairing a hole plug or ball mark on the Putting Green.

    d. Removing Loose Impediments when the ball is on the Putting Green.

    e. Marking or lifting a ball.

    f. Removing a Movable Obstruction.

    g. Lifting an interfering ball.

    h. Placing or replacing a ball as allowed by the Rules.

PROCEDURE WHEN YOUR BALL MOVES — AFTER YOU HAVE ADDRESSED YOUR BALL (RULE 18-2): When your ball is in a Sand Bunker or Water Hazard, you have Addressed Your Ball as soon as you have taken your stance. Outside a Sand Bunker or Water Hazard, you have Addressed Your Ball as soon as you have taken your stance and grounded your club. In both Stroke Play and Match Play, if your ball In Play is at rest and then moves to another spot after you Address it, but before you contact it during the downswing of your stroke, you will incur _a one-stroke penalty,_ even if you didn't do anything to cause the ball to move. You must then replace your ball before playing your next stroke, unless the movement of the ball occurs after you have begun your swing and you don't discontinue your swing.

PROCEDURE WHEN YOUR BALL MOVES — AFTER TOUCHING LOOSE IMPEDIMENTS (RULE 18-2): If your ball is at rest, you are permitted to remove Loose Impediments, such as twigs and leaves, _without penalty,_ except when both your ball and the Loose Impediments lie in or touch the same Sand Bunker or Water Hazard. If your ball is on the Putting Green and moves as a direct result of removing Loose Impediments, replace your ball, _without penalty._ If your ball is off the Putting Green and moves to another spot as a direct result of removing

Loose Impediments, or if you remove Loose Impediments within a club-length of your ball and it thereafter moves to another spot, you will incur *a one-stroke penalty.* You must then replace your ball before playing your next stroke, unless the movement of the ball occurs after you have begun your swing and you don't discontinue your swing.

PROCEDURE WHEN YOUR BALL IS MOVED BY YOUR FELLOW-COMPETITOR OR BY YOUR OPPONENT (RULE 18-3, 18-4):

In Stroke Play, if your ball is at rest, there is *no penalty* if it is touched or moved by your Fellow-Competitor, his caddie or equipment. Simply replace your ball. In Match Play, if your ball is at rest and then touched or moved by your Opponent, his caddie or equipment, you must replace your ball, *without penalty to you.* However, your Opponent will incur a *one-stroke penalty,* unless the touching or movement of your ball occurs when:

a. Searching for your ball; or

b. Playing a Wrong Ball; or

c. Measuring to determine which ball is furthest from the hole; or

d. Lifting a ball that might interfere with or assist play.

ADDITIONAL POINTERS: (1) If you accidentally move your ball or knock it off the tee before playing your first stroke on a hole, re-tee it, *without penalty*, and without counting any strokes, since your ball is not yet In Play. (2) If your ball is In Play and you accidentally touch it with your club, there is *no penalty* if your ball moves, as long as it only rocks, jiggles or oscillates and then settles back into its original position. (3) If you fail to replace your ball when required to do so after it has moved, there is generally *a two-stroke penalty* in Stroke Play, with no additional penalty for the ball movement, and *a loss of the hole* in Match Play. (4) If your ball is moved by the wind or water after it has come to rest and before you address it, play it where it comes to rest in its new location, *without penalty.* (5) When searching for your ball, let a non-partner drive the golf cart so neither of you will be penalized for moving your ball if the cart accidentally runs over it.

Dropping Your Ball

DROPPING YOUR BALL DEFINED: Under certain circumstances you will be required to put your ball In Play by dropping it within a certain area or by dropping it at a specific spot.

Wait, Mike! You have to stand erect...then you DROP your ball from shoulder height and at arm's length.

PROCEDURE FOR HOW TO DROP YOUR BALL (RULE 20-2): To properly drop your ball, you are required to stand erect, hold your ball at shoulder height and arm's length, and then release it. You may hold the ball in front of you or to your side at the time of the drop. The ball must first strike a part of the course where it is required to be dropped or it must be re-dropped. If the ball touches you or your equipment during the drop, you must re-drop it, *without penalty,* until it is dropped correctly. You will incur *a one-stroke penalty* in both Stroke Play and Match Play if you play a ball that has been dropped in an incorrect manner.

PROCEDURE FOR WHERE TO DROP YOUR BALL (RULE 20-2): When you are required to drop your ball as close to a specific spot as possible, your ball may not be dropped nearer to the hole than that specific spot. However, if you don't know the exact location of the spot, you may estimate its location. If you are required to drop your ball in a Sand Bunker or Water Hazard, it must be dropped in, and come to rest in, the Sand Bunker or Water Hazard. Refer to the section which deals with your particular situation when determining where to drop your ball.

PROCEDURE FOR WHEN TO RE-DROP YOUR BALL (RULE 20-2): You must re-drop your ball, *without penalty,* if you drop your ball and it:

1. Rolls more than two club-lengths away from where it first strikes a part of the course.

2. Rolls Out Of Bounds.

3. Rolls into a Hazard when dropped outside a Hazard.

4. Rolls out of a Hazard when dropped in a Hazard.

5. Rolls onto a Putting Green.

6. Rolls back into interference caused by Casual Water, Ground Under Repair, a Burrowing Animal Disturbance or an Immovable Obstruction when you are dropping from the same condition.

7. Rolls nearer the hole than its original position, unless otherwise permitted.

PROCEDURE FOR WHERE AND HOW TO RE-DROP YOUR BALL (RULE 20-2): When you are required to re-drop your ball, you must re-drop it at the same location where it was required to be dropped the first time. If, after a re-drop, the ball again rolls into any of the places mentioned in 1 through 7, do not drop the ball a third time. Instead, place the ball, by hand, as close as possible to the spot where the ball first struck a part of the course when it was re-dropped.

ADDITIONAL POINTERS: (1) Be careful when you drop your ball since you are not always entitled to a re-drop, _without penalty._ For example, if you take a drop from an Unplayable Lie and your ball rolls less than two club-lengths, no nearer the hole, and into another Unplayable Lie, you may not re-drop it _without penalty._ Instead you must again proceed under the Rules for an Unplayable Lie. (2) If you drop your ball in the wrong location but have not yet played a stroke at it from that location, you may re-drop it in the correct location, *without penalty.* (3) You may use any club to measure the one or two club-length distance within which to drop your ball. However, you must then use the same club when determining whether your ball has rolled more than two club-lengths away from where it first struck a part of the course. (4) No one else may drop your ball for you.

Lifting Your Ball

LIFTING YOUR BALL DEFINED: Under certain circumstances, the Rules permit you to pick up your ball, or Lift it, from the place where it is at rest. When your ball is at rest on the Putting Green, you may mark, lift and clean it at any time, except when another ball is in motion on the Putting Green.

PROCEDURE FOR LIFTING AND REPLACING A BALL (RULE 20-1, 20-3): When your ball is to be lifted under the Rules, it may be lifted by you or anyone you authorize. When an authorized person lifts your ball, you are responsible for any breach of the Rules. When your ball must be replaced, it need not be replaced by the person who marked and lifted it. However, it may only be replaced by you, your partner, or the person who lifted it. When a ball must be replaced, always mark its position before lifting it, or you will incur *a one-stroke penalty*.

PROCEDURE FOR LIFTING A BALL WHICH IS OFF THE PUTTING GREEN —TO DETERMINE ITS FITNESS OR IDENTITY (RULE 5-3, 12-2): You may lift your ball at any time to see if it is unfit for play. Your ball is considered unfit for play, and may be replaced, if it is visibly cut, cracked or out of shape, but not if it is just scuffed or marred. Similarly, you may lift what you *think* is your ball at any time to identify it, except when it is in a Sand Bunker or Water Hazard. Before lifting your ball when it's off the Putting Green, make sure you advise a Fellow-Competitor or Marker in Stroke Play, or an Opponent in Match Play, of your intention to lift it, give them an opportunity to watch, and then mark your ball before touching or lifting it. Failure to follow this pro-

cedure will result in *a one-stroke penalty*. If your ball is off the Putting Green when you lift it, you will also incur *a one-stroke penalty* if you clean your ball more than is necessary to identify it or if you clean it at all to check its fitness.

PROCEDURE FOR LIFTING A BALL WHICH IS OFF THE PUTTING GREEN TO PREVENT IT FROM ASSISTING OR INTERFERING WITH PLAY (RULE 22): Except when another ball is in motion, you may mark and then lift your ball, or have another ball marked and lifted, if you think the ball might assist or interfere with play. In Stroke Play, but not in Match Play, if you are asked to lift your assisting or interfering ball, you have the option of playing it rather than lifting it. You will incur *a one-stroke penalty* if you clean your assisting or interfering ball, except when it is lifted from the Putting Green.

Playing The Wrong Ball

PLAYING THE WRONG BALL DEFINED: You have Played A Wrong Ball when you have played a stroke at any ball other than (1) your ball In Play, (2) your Provisional Ball, or (3) your Second Ball, in Stroke Play, that is being played because you're unsure of your rights, or (4) your Second Ball, in Stroke Play, that is being played because your original ball was played from the wrong place.

I'm going to initial every ball so I don't ever hit a **WRONG BALL** again!

PROCEDURE WHEN YOU PLAY A WRONG BALL — FROM OUTSIDE A SAND BUNKER OR OUTSIDE A WATER HAZARD (RULE 15): In Stroke Play, you will incur *a two-stroke penalty* if you Play The Wrong Ball. Strokes played with the Wrong Ball are not counted. Thus, if you play three strokes with the original ball before Playing The Wrong Ball, you will be hitting six with the original ball when you discover your mistake, regardless of the number of strokes taken with the Wrong Ball. Once you discover that you're Playing The Wrong Ball you must correct your mistake by returning to the location of your original ball and completing the hole with it. If you begin play on the next hole without correcting your mistake, or if you leave the Putting Green on the final hole without declaring your intention to correct the mistake made on the final hole, you will be *disqualified*. In Match Play, the first player to Play A Wrong Ball *loses the hole*. If both you and your Opponent Play A Wrong Ball, and it can't be determined who was the first to do so, continue playing the hole with the Wrong Ball, *without penalty*.

PROCEDURE WHEN YOU PLAY A WRONG BALL — FROM A SAND BUNKER OR FROM A WATER HAZARD (RULE 15): There is *no penalty*, and you don't count any strokes taken, when you Play A Wrong Ball from a

Sand Bunker or from a Water Hazard. Simply replace the Wrong Ball in its original position in the Sand Bunker or Water Hazard and then continue play using your correct ball.

ADDITIONAL POINTERS: (1) Always put an identifying mark on your ball so you won't accidentally hit another player's ball. (2) If your first stroke from the Teeing Ground is played with a ball that belongs to someone else and you finish the hole with it, you have not Played A Wrong Ball since a ball played from the Teeing Ground into the hole is not a Wrong Ball, even if it does not belong to you.

Searching For Your Ball

SEARCHING FOR YOUR BALL DEFINED: When you hit your ball and can't find it, you are allowed to search for it for a maximum of five minutes before it becomes a Lost Ball.

PROCEDURE FOR SEARCHING FOR YOUR BALL —
OUTSIDE A SAND BUNKER AND OUTSIDE A WATER
HAZARD (RULE 12-1): When searching for your ball outside a Sand Bunker or Water Hazard, you may touch or bend long grass, bushes, and other vegetation, but only

to the extent necessary to find and identify your ball. If you, your partner, or your caddies cause your ball to move during the search, you must replace it and take *a one-stroke penalty*, unless the ball is in a Sand Bunker, a Water Hazard, Casual Water, Ground Under Repair or a Burrowing Animal Disturbance. In addition, if you improve your lie, your line of play, or the area of your intended swing during your search activity, you will incur *a two-stroke penalty* in Stroke Play, and *a loss of the hole* in Match Play.

Careful, Barb... you're not allowed to LIFT your ball from the HAZARD to IDENTIFY it!

PROCEDURE FOR SEARCHING FOR YOUR BALL — IN A SAND BUNKER OR WATER HAZARD (RULE 12-1): When searching for your ball in a Sand Bunker or Water Hazard, you may remove sand and Loose Impediments by using your hand, your club, a rake or various other means. If your ball moves during your search, simply replace it before playing, *without penalty*. Since there is *no penalty* for playing a Wrong Ball from a Sand Bunker or a Water Hazard, you should remove only enough sand or enough Loose Impediments to see a portion of a ball. You are not permitted to lift the ball in order to identify it as your own ball. If you remove an excess of material, there is no penalty as long as you recover the ball so only a portion of it is visible. If, after hitting out of the Sand Bunker or Water Hazard, you discover that the ball you played is not your own, replace it, *without penalty,* and don't count any strokes played with it from the Hazard. Then proceed to look for your ball.

ADDITIONAL POINTERS: (1) If you accidentally move your ball during your search for it when it is lying in water in a Water Hazard, or during your search for it when it is in Casual Water, Ground Under Repair or in a Burrowing Animal Disturbance, there is *no penalty.* Simply replace it or proceed with the other options of

SEARCHING FOR BALL

play that are available in those situations. (2) You will incur *a one-stroke penalty* in both Stroke Play and Match Play if you lift a ball from a Sand Bunker or Water Hazard to identify it.

Cleaning Your Ball

PROCEDURE FOR CLEANING YOUR BALL (RULE 21):
You will incur *a one-stroke penalty* if you clean your ball when it is not permitted. When your ball is at rest, you are permitted to mark, lift and then clean your ball as follows:

1. *On The Putting Green:* You may clean your ball *without penalty.*

2. *Off The Putting Green:* You may clean your ball, *without penalty,* when the Rules permit you to *lift* your ball. Exceptions:

a. When you *lift* your ball to identify it, you may clean it, but only to the extent necessary to identify it.

b. When you *lift* your ball to determine its fitness for play or when you *lift* it to prevent it from assisting or interfering with play, you may not clean it.

ADDITIONAL POINTERS: (1) Although not recommended, you are permitted to clean your ball by rubbing it on the Putting Green, as long as such rubbing is not done for the purpose of testing the surface of the Putting Green.

Putting Green

ON THE PUTTING GREEN DEFINED: The Putting Green is that part of the course that is specially prepared for Putting. It does not include the short grass around it that is often called the _apron,_ the _fringe_ or the _collar._ A ball is On The Putting Green when any part of the ball touches the Putting Green.

PROCEDURES REGARDING THE LINE OF PUTT (RULE 16-1): It is _a two-stroke penalty_ in Stroke Play, and _a loss of the hole_ in Match Play, to:

1. Use anything other than your hand or golf club to move or remove sand, loose soil, or other Loose Impediments from your Line of Putt on the Putting Green. Note that sand and loose soil may not be moved or removed from the apron, fringe or collar because sand and loose soil are only Loose Impediments when on the Putting Green.

2. Repair irregularities on your Line Of Putt, including raised tufts of grass or spike marks. Exception: You may repair any damage on your Line Of Putt which has been caused by the impact of a ball or by the plugging of a former hole, even if your ball is not yet on the surface of the Putting Green.

3. Allow your partner or your caddies to stand on or close to an extension of the Line Of Putt behind the ball while you are putting.

4. Roll a ball on the Putting Green to test the surface or determine the break of the Putt.

5. Brush aside dew which is on your Line Of Putt since dew is not Casual Water or a Loose Impediment.

6. Allow your partner or your caddies to touch the Putting Green to indicate your Line Of Putt when your ball is on the Putting Green.

7. Putt from the wrong location. If you move your ball-marker one or more clubhead-lengths so it will not interfere with the play, stance or stroke of another player, make sure to return the ball-marker to its original position before replacing and then Putting your ball or you will be Putting from the wrong location.

8. Putt croquet style, where one leg is on each side of the Line Of Putt, or Putt with either foot touching the Line Of Putt or an extension of the line behind the ball.

PROCEDURES REGARDING THE FLAGSTICK (RULE 17): It is _a two-stroke penalty_ in Stroke Play, and _the loss of the hole_ in Match Play, to:

1. Strike the Flagstick with your ball when you play a stroke from anywhere on the Putting Green.

2. Strike an _attended_ Flagstick with your ball when you play a stroke from anywhere off the Putting Green.

3. Authorize the removal of an *unattended* Flagstick while your ball is moving.

4. Touch the Line Of Putt on the Putting Green with the Flagstick.

5. Have someone indicate your line of play by holding the Flagstick in the air, away from the hole, while you make your stroke. Note: The Flagstick may be held in the air, *at the hole,* by your partner or caddie, while you make your stroke.

— 94 —

PROCEDURE WHEN YOUR BALL IS OVERHANGING THE HOLE (RULE 16-2): If any part of your ball is hanging over the lip of the cup, you are given enough time to reach the hole without unreasonable delay. You then have ten seconds to determine if your ball is _at rest._ If your ball falls into the hole before the ten-second period has passed, there is no extra stroke. If your ball falls into the hole after the ten-second period has passed, add one stroke to your score.

PROCEDURE WHEN YOUR BALL IS ON THE WRONG PUTTING GREEN [RULE 25-3]: If your ball comes to rest on the Putting Green of a hole other than the one you're playing, lift, clean and then drop your ball, *without penalty,* within one club-length of the nearest spot off the Putting Green, no nearer the hole you're playing, and not in a Sand Bunker or Water Hazard.

PROCEDURE WHEN YOU FAIL TO HOLE OUT [RULE 3-2]: In Stroke Play competition, if you fail to hole out on any hole, you will be *disqualified* unless you correct your mistake before playing a stroke on the next hole, or, if it's the last hole, before leaving the Putting Green of the last hole.

ADDITIONAL POINTERS: (1) When your ball is at rest on the Putting Green, you may mark, lift and clean it. (2) If your ball moves and comes to rest in another location when you accidentally touch it with your putter, before playing a stroke, you must replace the ball and take *a one-stroke penalty.* (3) There is no penalty if you Putt with one hand while holding the Flagstick with the other hand, as long as your ball doesn't strike the flagstick.

Advice

ADVICE DEFINED: Advice is defined as any counsel or suggestion which could influence you in determining (1) your play, (2) the choice of a club, or (3) the method of making a stroke.

PROCEDURE FOR ASKING FOR — OR GIVING — ADVICE (RULE 8): You will incur *a two-stroke penalty* in Stroke Play, and *a loss of the hole* in Match Play, if you ask for Advice from anyone except your partners or your caddies, or if you give Advice to anyone other than

your partner during a round. The following are examples of what is, and is not, permitted during a round:

1. You are not permitted to give Advice to, or receive Advice from, anyone other than your partner or your caddies about how to swing a club or what club to use for a specific shot. However, if you want to find out what clubs your Opponents or Fellow-Competitors are using, you may look into their golf bags.

2. You are permitted to ask anyone questions, or answer questions, about the Rules of Golf.

3. You are permitted to ask or answer questions about matters of public information such as the position of the Flagstick on the Putting Green or the distance from a permanent object, such as a tree, to the middle of the Putting Green. However, you are not permitted to ask anyone, other than your partner or your caddies, about the distance from a non-permanent object, such as your own ball, to another object.

4. When your ball is off the Putting Green, anyone may indicate the line of play to you, but no one may stand on or close to the line, or leave any indicator on it while you are playing the stroke, except the flag may be held up at the hole.

5. When your ball is on the Putting Green, and before you attempt a stroke, your partners and your caddies may indicate your Line Of Putt, but no one may touch your Line or leave a mark on it.

Four-Ball Competitions

FOUR-BALL COMPETITION DEFINED: In Four-Ball Stroke Play and Four-Ball Match Play, players form two person teams. Each player plays his own ball on each hole. The lower score of the two partners is the team's score for the hole.

PROCEDURE TO DETERMINE WHEN PARTNERS ARE PENALIZED DURING FOUR-BALL COMPETITION (RULE 30, 31): When a player incurs a penalty for breach of a Rule, the player's partner is not also penalized unless the player's breach assists the partner. In addition, in Four-Ball Match Play, if a player's breach adversely affects an Opponent's play, both the player breaching the Rule and the player's partner are penalized.

ADDITIONAL POINTERS: (1) When it is a player's turn to play, the player's partner may play first, even though the player's partner may be closer to the hole than any other player. (2) If either partner carries more than fourteen clubs, both partners will be penalized. (3) If a player plays a stroke with a Wrong Ball, the player's partner will not be penalized, even if the Wrong Ball belongs to the player's partner. (4) In Four-Ball Match

F
O
U
R
-
B
A
L
L
C
O
M
P
E
T
I
T
I
O
N

Play, when the penalty for breach of a Rule is a loss of the hole, the player committing the breach will be disqualified from playing the hole.

Practicing On The Course

PROCEDURE FOR PRACTICING ON THE COURSE —
BEFORE THE START OF A COMPETITION (RULE 7-1): When
you are in a Stroke Play competition, you will be _disqualified_ if you practice on the course or test the surface
of any Putting Green on the course before starting play
that day. Exception: You may practice chipping or
putting on or near the first Teeing Ground. When two or
more rounds of a Stroke Play competition are to be
played over consecutive days, you are prohibited from
practicing on the course between rounds. In Match Play,
you may practice anywhere on the course before the
start of the match, _without penalty._

PROCEDURE FOR PRACTICING ON THE COURSE —
DURING A COMPETITION (RULE 7-2): You will incur _a_
two-stroke penalty in Stroke Play, and _the loss of the_
hole in Match Play, if you play a practice stroke on the
course during the play of a hole or between the play of
two holes. Exception: You may practice putting or chipping on or near the Putting Green of the hole last played
or on the Teeing Ground of the next hole to be played, as
long as this practice is not from a Sand Bunker or Water
Hazard and does not unduly delay play.

ADDITIONAL POINTERS: (1) Even though you may be penalized for practicing on the course or for playing a practice *stroke*, a practice *swing* may be taken at any time since you are not attempting to strike a ball while practice *swinging*. (2) If you are penalized for practicing on the course *between the play of two holes,* the penalty applies to the next hole rather than the one you just played.

Striking The Ball More Than Once

PROCEDURE WHEN YOU STRIKE THE BALL MORE THAN ONCE (RULE 14-4): If your club strikes the ball two or more times while making one stroke, count it as *two strokes in total,* one stroke for the swing at the ball plus *one penalty stroke.*

Staked Trees

Young trees are often staked or otherwise identified in order to protect them. Typically, Local Rules provide that if a staked tree interferes with your stance or the area of your intended swing, you may lift, clean and then drop your ball, *without penalty,* within one club-length of the *nearest point of relief,* no nearer the hole and not in a Water Hazard, a Sand Bunker or on a Putting Green. Note that the *nearest point of relief* is the closest spot, no nearer the hole, where you can take your stance without the tree interfering with your ball, feet or swing. This *nearest point* may result in the tree being directly between your ball and the target. As with Immovable Obstructions, there is no relief if the staked tree only interferes with your line of play.

Winter Rules

I): When adverse weather affects the playing conditions of a course, local Winter Rules may permit you to move your ball to *preferred lies.* Since Winter Rules differ from course to course, they should be in writing and posted. Often, Winter Rules provide that a ball at rest on the fairway may be lifted, cleaned and then placed, *without penalty.* The ball must usually be placed within one club-length, no nearer the hole, at a location which duplicates as nearly as possible the stance required to be played by the original lie. Before playing a course where Winter Rules are in effect, determine:

1. If the lie of your ball may be improved in the fairway only,

2. If your ball may be cleaned when lifted, and

3. The distance your ball may be moved from its original location at rest.

Glossary

ADDRESSING THE BALL: When your ball is outside a Sand Bunker or Water Hazard, you have Addressed The Ball when you have taken a stance and grounded your club behind the ball. When your ball is in a Sand Bunker or Water Hazard, you are not permitted to Ground Your Club, and thus, you have Addressed The Ball as soon as you have taken a stance.

BALL IN PLAY: Your ball is In Play as soon as you make a Stroke from the Teeing Ground. Your ball continues to be In Play until it is holed out unless it is: (1) Lost, (2) Out Of Bounds, (3) Lifted, or (4) Replaced by another ball which has been substituted under an applicable Rule.

COMPETITOR: Anyone playing in a Stroke Play competition is a Competitor.

FELLOW-COMPETITOR: Anyone playing in a Stroke Play competition, in your same group, is your Fellow-Competitor.

FOUR-BALL COMPETITION: In Four-Ball Stroke Play and Four-Ball Match Play, two players act as a team and play their better ball against the better ball of another team of two players.

LINE OF PLAY: Your Line Of Play is the direction you want your ball to travel. It includes a reasonable distance on each side of the intended direction, extends vertically upwards from the ground, but does not go beyond the hole.

LINE OF PUTT: Your Line Of Putt is the direction you want your ball to travel on the Putting Green. It includes a reasonable distance on each side of the intended direction, but it does not go beyond the hole.

MARGIN: The Margin is a real or imagined line that defines an area of the course, such as a Water Hazard or Ground Under Repair.

MARKER: A Marker records the score of a Competitor in a Stroke Play competition. The Marker is often a Fellow-Competitor.

MATCH PLAY: Match Play is a competition based on the number of holes won, rather than the strokes played.

OPPONENT: The person or side you are competing against in Match Play is your Opponent.

OUTSIDE AGENCY: An Outside Agency is a person or thing that is not part of the match in Match Play, and a person or thing that is not part of the Competitor's side in Stroke Play. Examples of Outside Agencies include animals, birds, inanimate objects, referees, markers and spectators. Wind and water are not Outside Agencies.

PROVISIONAL BALL: A Provisional Ball is a ball that is played in order to save time when there is a reasonable possibility that your original ball is Out Of Bounds or is Lost *outside* a Water Hazard.

RUB OF THE GREEN: A Rub Of The Green occurs when your ball in motion is accidentally deflected or stopped by an Outside Agency.

SECOND BALL: In Stroke Play, if a competitor is uncertain about the proper way to proceed in a situation, a Second Ball may be played on the hole in addition to the ball In Play. Thereafter, a ruling must be obtained to determine which of the two balls was played pursuant to the Rules.

STROKE: A Stroke occurs when you make a *forward* movement of your club with the intention of fairly striking at and moving the ball. If you intentionally stop your downswing before the clubhead reaches your ball, you have not made a Stroke.

STROKE PLAY: Stroke Play is a competition based on the total number of strokes played, rather than the number of holes won. Stroke Play is also known as Medal Play.

TAKING A STANCE: You have Taken A Stance when you have placed your feet in position in preparation for making a Stroke.

THROUGH THE GREEN: Through The Green is the entire area of the golf course except for all the Sand Bunkers on the course, all the Water Hazards on the course, the Teeing Ground of the hole being played, and the Putting Green of the hole being played.

Index